Getting to Know You

201 Fun Questions to Deepen Your Relationship and Hear Each Other's Story

Jeffrey Mason

INTRODUCTION

"As soon as I saw you, I knew an adventure
was going to happen." — Winnie the Pooh

Relationships are as different as the individuals involved.

Many are just starting, with that potent excitement of
newness and getting to know each other.

Others are years long, with that comfortable intertwining
of habits and routines.

Whatever the number of days, months, and years you
have known each other, there will always be new things
to know and learn.

And that is where the magic of romance is made and
sustained.

Think back to when you first met. Remember how the
days and nights were filled with new discoveries, new
understandings? Each new fact and insight gained was
fuel for the flames of your growing closeness and
romance.

Talking and sharing and learning about each other's life
story builds the understanding and intimacy that are the
foundations of fun and lasting connections.

Getting to Know You has been crafted by the creators of
the popular **Hear Your Story** line of books to provide
every couple with a path to more talking, learning,
sharing, hearing, and understanding.

Whether your relationship is weeks or years old, the
questions within these pages will create fun, closeness,
and discovery for both of you while also strengthening
and deepening your bond.

IN THE BEGINNING
"one's not half of two; two are halves of one."
– E.E. Cummings

Person A

When were you born?

_____

What was your full name at birth?

_____

Were you named after a relative or someone else of significance?

_____

In what city were you born?

_____

Were you born in a hospital? If not, where?

_____

_____

What was your height (length) and weight at birth?

_____

How old were your parents when you were born?

_____

_____

IN THE BEGINNING

"Sometimes I catch myself smiling because I am thinking of you."
— Unknown

Person B

When were you born?

_____

What was your full name at birth?

_____

Were you named after a relative or someone else of significance?

_____

Where were you born?

_____

Were you born in a hospital? If not, where?

_____

_____

What was your height (length) and weight at birth?

_____

How old were your parents when you were born?

_____

_____

IN THE BEGINNING
"Do not dare not to dare."
— C.S. Lewis
Person A

How many siblings do you have?

_____

Were you the oldest, middle, or youngest child?

_____

What were your first words?

_____

How old were you when you started to walk?

_____

What story have you been told about the day you were born?

_____

_____

_____

_____

_____

_____

IN THE BEGINNING

"To get the full value of joy, you must have someone to divide it with." — Mark Twain

Person B

How many siblings do you have?

_____

Were you the oldest, middle, or youngest child?

_____

What were your first words?

_____

How old were you when you started to walk?

_____

What story have you been told about the day you were born?

_____

_____

_____

_____

_____

_____

TRIVIA

"If you wish to be loved, love."
— Lucius Annaeus Seneca

Person A

Rollercoasters: Yes or No?

_____

Where would you live if money were not a concern?

_____

_____

Do you still have your tonsils?

_____

Have you ever broken a bone?

_____

What superpower would you pick for yourself?

_____

_____

What is your go-to late night snack?

_____

What is your shoe size?

_____

TRIVIA

"If you look for it, I've got a sneaky feeling
you'll find that love actually is all around." — *Love, Actually*

Person B

Rollercoasters: Yes or No?

_____

Where would you live if money were not a concern?

_____

_____

Do you still have your tonsils?

_____

Have you ever broken a bone?

_____

What superpower would you pick for yourself?

_____

_____

How old were you when you started to walk?

_____

What is your shoe size?

_____

GROWING UP
"Growing old is mandatory; growing up is optional."
— Chili Davis
Person A

What three words best describe you when you were a kid?

_____

_____

_____

Did you have a nickname when you were growing up?
How did you get it?

_____

_____

Who was your best friend when you were a kid? Are you
still in contact with them?

_____

_____

What television family most reminds you of yours?

_____

Did you ever meet your great-grandparents?

_____

_____

GROWING UP

"At twenty years of age, the will reigns; at thirty,
the wit; and at forty, the judgment. — Benjamin Franklin

Person B

What three words best describe you when you were a kid?

_____

_____

_____

Did you have a nickname when you were growing up?
How did you get it?

_____

_____

Who was your best friend when you were a kid? Are you
still in contact with them?

_____

_____

What television family most reminds you of yours?

_____

Did you ever meet your great-grandparents?

_____

_____

GROWING UP

"Even though you're growing up, you
should never stop having fun." — Nina Dobrev

Person A

Did you have braces? If yes, how old were you when you got them?

_____

When you were a kid, did you share a bedroom or have one to yourself?

_____

What were your regular chores when you were growing up?

_____

_____

_____

Did you get an allowance? If yes, how much?

_____

_____

What is one thing you miss about being a kid?

_____

_____

_____

GROWING UP

"Someday, you will be old enough to
start reading fairy tales again." — C.S. Lewis

Person B

Did you have braces? If yes, how old were you when you
got them?

_____

When you were a kid, did you share a bedroom or have
one to yourself?

_____

What were your regular chores when you were growing up?

_____

_____

_____

Did you get an allowance? If yes, how much?

_____

_____

What is one thing you miss about being a kid?

_____

_____

_____

TRIVIA

"Love is composed of a single soul inhabiting two bodies."
— Aristotle

Person A

Do you have a library card?

_____

Do you read your horoscope?

_____

Do you buy lottery tickets?

_____

Were you a scout?

_____

What is your biggest fear?

_____

Do you have any allergies? If yes, what are they?

_____

_____

What would be the title of your autobiography?

_____

_____

TRIVIA

"And remember, as it was written, to love another person is to see the face of God." — Victor Hugo, Les Misérables

Person B

Do you have a library card?

_____

Do you read your horoscope?

_____

Do you buy lottery tickets?

_____

Were you a scout?

_____

What is your biggest fear?

_____

Do you have any allergies? If yes, what are they?

_____

_____

What would be the title of your autobiography?

_____

_____

THE TEEN YEARS

"As a teenager you are at the last stage in your life when you will be happy to hear that the phone is for you." — Fran Leibowitz

Person A

What three words describe you as a teenager?

_____

_____

_____

How did you dress and style your hair during your teens?

_____

_____

_____

How old were you when you got your driver's license and who taught you to drive?

_____

What was a common weekend night like during your teens?

_____

_____

_____

_____

THE TEEN YEARS

"Live your life like you are 80 years old looking
back on your teenage years." — Taylor Swift

Person B

What three words describe you as a teenager?

_____

_____

_____

How did you dress and style your hair during your teens?

_____

_____

_____

How old were you when you got your driver's license and
who taught you to drive?

_____

What was your social life like during your high school?

_____

_____

_____

_____

THE TEEN YEARS

"The greatest thing you will ever learn is to just love
and be loved in return." — Nat King Cole, *Nature Boy*

Person A

Did you have a curfew?

_____

How much did you date when you were in high school?

_____

_____

Who did you eat lunch with?

_____

_____

What school activities or sports did you participate in?

_____

_____

_____

What were your favorite and least favorite subjects?

_____

_____

THE TEEN YEARS

"Teenagers have growing pains...and are growing pains."
— Unknown

Person B

Did you have a curfew?

_____

How much did you date when you were in high school?

_____

_____

Who did you eat lunch with?

_____

_____

What school activities or sports did you participate in?

_____

_____

_____

_____

What were your favorite and least favorite subjects?

_____

_____

THE TEEN YEARS

"Telling a teenager, the facts of life is like
giving a fish a bath." — Arnold H. Glasow

Person A

What was your relationship with your parents like during
your teen years?

_____

_____

_____

_____

Is there a teacher, coach, or other mentor who had a
significant impact on you when you were growing up?
What was their biggest influence?

_____

_____

_____

_____

_____

_____

THE TEEN YEARS

"Adolescence is just one big walking pimple."
— Carol Burnett

Person B

What was your relationship with your parents like during your teen years?

_____

_____

_____

_____

Is there a teacher, coach, or other mentor who had a significant impact on you when you were growing up? What was their biggest influence?

_____

_____

_____

_____

_____

_____

_____

WHERE HAVE YOU LIVED?

"Everything you can imagine is real"
— Pablo Picasso

Person A

List the cities you have lived in during your lifetime.

1. _____

2. _____

3. _____

4. _____

5. _____

6. _____

7. _____

8. _____

9. _____

10. _____

WHERE HAVE YOU LIVED?

"You have bewitched my body and soul, and I love,
I love, I love you." — Jane Austen, *Pride & Prejudice*

Person B

List the cities you have lived in during your lifetime.

1. _____

2. _____

3. _____

4. _____

5. _____

6. _____

7. _____

8. _____

9. _____

10. _____

FAVORITE THINGS

"We loved with a love that was more than love."
— Edgar Allan Poe

Person A

What is your favorite color?

_____

Dogs or cats?

_____

What is your favorite way to get some exercise?

_____

What is your favorite way to relax?

_____

Mornings or nights?

_____

What is a favorite moment from the last twelve months?

_____

_____

_____

Do you have a favorite item of clothing?

_____

_____

FAVORITE THINGS

"The real voyage of discovery consists not in seeking
new landscapes, but in having new eyes." — Marcel Proust

Person B

What is your favorite color?

_____

Dogs or cats?

_____

What is your favorite way to get some exercise?

_____

What is your favorite way to relax?

_____

Mornings or nights?

_____

What is a favorite moment from the last twelve months?

_____

_____

_____

Do you have a favorite item of clothing?

_____

_____

CUPID TALK

"I saw that you were perfect, and so I loved you. Then I saw that you were not perfect, and I loved you even more." — Angelita Lim

Person A

Do you believe in love at first sight?

_____

Do you believe in soulmates?

_____

How old were you when you had your first kiss?

_____

How old were you when you had your first date?

_____

What did you do on that date?

_____

_____

Did you have any serious relationships in high school?

_____

List three creative ideas you would enjoy doing on a date.

_____

_____

_____

CUPID TALK

"A real friend is one who walks in when the
rest of the world walks out." — Walter Winchell

Person B

Do you believe in love at first sight?

_____

Do you believe in soulmates?

_____

How old were you when you had your first kiss?

_____

How old were you when you had your first date?

_____

What did you do on that date?

_____

_____

Did you have any serious relationships in high school?

_____

List three creative ideas you would enjoy doing on a date.

_____

_____

_____

CUPID TALK

"The best thing to hold on to in life is each other."
— Audrey Hepburn

Person A

Have you ever written someone a love poem or song?

_____

If yes, write a few lines that you may remember.

_____

_____

_____

_____

What are five things you consider to be romantic.

_____

_____

_____

_____

_____

What is your opinion of Valentine's Day?

_____

_____

CUPID TALK

*"Yes, I'm drunk. And you're beautiful. And tomorrow morning,
I'll be sober, but you'll still be beautiful." — The Dreamers*

Person B

Have you ever written someone a love poem or song?

_____

If yes, write a few lines that you may remember.

_____

_____

_____

_____

What are five things you consider to be romantic.

_____

_____

_____

_____

_____

What is your opinion of Valentine's Day?

_____

_____

CUPID TALK

"You know you're in love when you can't fall asleep because
reality is finally better than your dreams." — Dr. Seuss

Person A

What are the five most important qualities of a successful
relationship?

_____

_____

_____

_____

_____

What are your top five relationship deal breakers?

_____

_____

_____

_____

_____

What is your favorite thing that I do for you?

_____

_____

CUPID TALK

"Forgiveness is the oil of all relationships."
— Unknown

Person B

What are the five most important qualities of a successful relationship?

_____

_____

_____

_____

_____

What are your top five relationship deal breakers?

_____

_____

_____

_____

_____

What is your favorite thing that I do for you?

_____

_____

FAVORITE THINGS
"Courage is not the absence of fear, but the mastery of it."
— Mark Twain
Person A

What is your favorite flavor of ice cream?

_____

What is your favorite kind of cookie?

_____

Which is your favorite holiday?

_____

What is your favorite movie quote?

_____

_____

What is your favorite season of the year?

_____

What is your favorite snack?

_____

What is a favorite family tradition from your childhood?

_____

_____

_____

FAVORITE THINGS

"Being deeply loved by someone gives you strength,
while loving someone deeply gives you courage." — Lao-Tzu

Person B

What is your favorite flavor of ice cream?

_____

What is your favorite kind of cookie?

_____

Which is your favorite holiday?

_____

What is your favorite movie quote?

_____

_____

What is your favorite season of the year?

_____

What is your favorite snack?

_____

What is a favorite family tradition from your childhood?

_____

_____

_____

YOUR PARENTS

"All that I am, or hope to be, I owe to my mother."
— Abraham Lincoln

Person A

How did your parents meet?

_____

_____

What were their occupations?

_____

_____

_____

In three words, describe your parent's relationship.

_____

_____

_____

Did either of them have any unique talents?

_____

_____

_____

YOUR PARENTS

"A father carries pictures where his money used to be."
— Steve Martin

Person B

How did your parents meet?

_____

_____

What were their occupations?

_____

_____

_____

In three words, describe your parent's relationship.

_____

_____

_____

Did either of them have any unique talents?

_____

_____

_____

YOUR PARENTS

"If at first you don't succeed, try doing it the way
mom told you to it in the beginning." — Unknown

Person A

Where was your mother born and where did she grow up?

_____

_____

What three words would you use to describe her?

_____

_____

_____

In what three ways are you most like your mother?

_____

_____

_____

In what ways are the two of you different?

_____

_____

_____

YOUR PARENTS

"Sweater, n.: garment worn by a child when
its mother is feeling chilly." — Ambrose Pierce

Person B

Where was your mother born and where did she grow up?

_____

_____

What three words would you use to describe her?

_____

_____

_____

In what three ways are you most like your mother?

_____

_____

_____

In what ways are the two of you different?

_____

_____

_____

YOUR PARENTS

"My father didn't tell me how to live. He lived
and let me watch him do it." — Clarence Budington Kelland

Person A

Where was your father born and where did he grow up?

_____

_____

What three words would you use to describe him?

_____

_____

_____

In what three ways are you most like your father?

_____

_____

_____

In what ways are the two of you different?

_____

_____

_____

YOUR PARENTS

"The older I get, the smarter my father seems to get."
— Tim Russert

Person B

Where was your father born and where did he grow up?

_____

_____

What three words would you use to describe him?

_____

_____

In what three ways are you most like your father?

_____

_____

In what ways are the two of you different?

_____

_____

_____

FAVORITE THINGS

"Love isn't hopeless. Look, maybe I'm no expert on the subject, but there was one time I got it right." — *The Simpsons*

Person A

What is your favorite kind of weather?

_____

What do you usually order to drink at a restaurant or bar?

_____

What is a favorite toy from your childhood?

_____

What is your favorite type of food (Thai, Mexican, etc.)?

_____

What is your favorite restaurant?

_____

What is a favorite quote?

_____

_____

What is your favorite way to cheer yourself up?

_____

_____

_____

FAVORITE THINGS

"My favorite things in life don't cost any money. It's really clear that the most precious resource we all have is time." — Steve Jobs

Person B

What is your favorite kind of weather?

_____

What do you usually order to drink at a restaurant or bar?

_____

What is a favorite toy from your childhood?

_____

What is your favorite type of food (Thai, Mexican, etc.)?

_____

What is your favorite restaurant?

_____

What is a favorite quote?

_____

_____

What is your favorite way to cheer yourself up?

_____

_____

_____

SPIRITUALITY & RELIGION
"Everything will be ok in the end. If it's not ok, it's not the end."
— John Lennon

Person A

What do you believe is the purpose of life?

_____

_____

_____

_____

Which has the most impact on our lives: fate or free will?

_____

_____

When you were growing up, were your parents religious?

_____

How did they express their spiritual beliefs?

_____

_____

_____

_____

SPIRITUALITY & RELIGION

"One day your life will flash before your eyes.
Make sure it's worth watching." — *The Bucket List*

Person B

What do you believe is the purpose of life?

_____

_____

_____

_____

_____

Which has the most impact on our lives: fate or free will?

_____

_____

When you were growing up, were your parents religious?

_____

How did they express their spiritual beliefs?

_____

_____

_____

_____

SPIRITUALITY & RELIGION

"Love's gift cannot be given; it waits to be accepted."
— Rabindranath Tagore

Person A

How have your religious beliefs and practices changed over the course of your life?

_____

_____

_____

_____

Do you pray? If yes, when, and how often?

_____

_____

What role does religion have in your life?

_____

_____

_____

_____

SPIRITUALITY & RELIGION

"True love begins when nothing is looked for in return."
— Antoine de Saint-Exupery

Person B

How have your religious beliefs and practices changed over the course of your life?

_____

_____

_____

_____

_____

Do you pray? If yes, when, and how often?

_____

_____

What role does religion have in your life?

_____

_____

_____

_____

_____

TRIVIA
"We are asleep until we fall in love!
— Leo Tolstoy, War and Peace
Person A

What is your typical breakfast?

_____

_____

What is your biggest big pet peeve?

_____

Which do you prefer: a large party or a small gathering?

_____

How many speeding tickets have you received?

_____

What is your typical order at a coffeehouse?

_____

Do you remember your dreams?

_____

What would you do if you could do any one thing for a day?

_____

_____

_____

TRIVIA

"Loving you is my greatest strength and my biggest weakness."
— Unknown

Person B

What is your typical breakfast?

_____

_____

What is your biggest big pet peeve?

_____

Which do you prefer: a large party or a small gathering?

_____

How many speeding tickets have you received?

_____

What is your typical order at a coffeehouse?

_____

Do you remember your dreams?

_____

What would you do if you could do any one thing for a day?

_____

_____

_____

WORK & CAREER
"Be yourself; everyone else is already taken."
— Oscar Wilde
Person A

When you were a kid, what did you want to be when you "grew up?"

_____

_____

_____

Is there a job or profession your parents wanted you to pursue?

_____

If you could do any profession, what would it be?

_____

_____

Have you ever wanted to own your own business? If yes, what kind of business would it be?

_____

_____

What was your first job? How old were you

_____

WORK & CAREER

"You can't build a reputation on what you're going to do."
— Confucius

Person B

When you were a kid, what did you want to be when you "grew up?"

_____

_____

_____

Is there a job or profession your parents wanted you to pursue?

_____

If you could do any profession, what would it be?

_____

_____

Have you ever wanted to own your own business? If yes, what kind of business would it be?

_____

_____

What was your first job? How old were you

_____

WORK & CAREER

*"I'm a great believer in luck, and I find the harder
I work, the more I have of it." — Thomas Jefferson*

Person A

What are the favorite and least favorite jobs you have had?

_____

_____

What are your career goals and what are you currently
doing to achieve them?

_____

_____

_____

Would you move to another part of the country if it would
help you partner's career?

_____

How do you create boundaries between your work and
home lives?

_____

_____

_____

WORK & CAREER

"Do not be too timid and squeamish about your actions.
All life is an experiment." — Ralph Waldo Emerson

Person B

What are the favorite and least favorite jobs you have had?

_____

_____

What are your career goals and what are you currently
doing to achieve them?

_____

_____

_____

_____

Would you move to another part of the country if it would
help you partner's career?

_____

How do you create boundaries between your work and
home lives?

_____

_____

_____

TRIVIA

"If I had a flower for every time I thought of you...
I could walk through my garden forever." — Alfred Tennyson

Person A

What name would you pick if you had to change your first name?

_____

What is a personal accomplishment you are proud of?

_____

_____

_____

If you could only eat three things for the next year, with no harm to your health, what would they be?

_____

_____

_____

Who is your celebrity crush?

_____

Were you ever in a relationship with someone your parents didn't like?

_____

TRIVIA

"I love her and that's the beginning and end of everything."
— F. Scott Fitzgerald, *The Great Gatsby*

Person B

What name would you pick if you had to change your first name?

_____

What is a personal accomplishment you are proud of?

_____

_____

_____

If you could only eat three things for the next year, with no harm to your health, what would they be?

_____

_____

_____

Who is your celebrity crush?

_____

Were you ever in a relationship with someone your parents didn't like?

_____

MONEY STUFF

"If you want to know what God thinks of money,
just look at the people he gave it to." — Dorothy Parker

Person A

Do you use a budget to manage your spending?

_____

What percentage of your income do you save and invest?

_____

Should a couple in a long-term committed relationship
have joint or separate bank accounts?

_____

Do you pay off your credit cards each month?

_____

What are you currently doing to save for retirement?

_____

_____

If you won $1 million dollars in the lottery, what are the
first three things you would do with the money?

_____

_____

_____

MONEY STUFF

"The man who does more than he is paid for will soon be paid for more than he does." — Napoleon Hill

Person B

Do you use a budget to manage your spending?

_____

What percentage of your income do you save and invest?

_____

Should a couple in a long-term committed relationship have joint or separate bank accounts?

_____

Do you pay off your credit cards each month?

_____

What are you currently doing to save for retirement?

_____

_____

If you won $1 million dollars in the lottery, what are the first three things you would do with the money?

_____

_____

_____

MONEY STUFF

"Wealth consists not in having great possessions, but in having few wants" — Epictetus

Person A

Are you comfortable talking about money?

_____

What is your opinion of prenuptial agreements?

_____

What was your last big purchase? Was it worth it?

_____

Would you rather spend money on experiences or things?

_____

Are you able to donate to nonprofits?

_____

Do you save for big purchases or use credit?

_____

What was your family's financial situation when you were a kid? How has that influenced how you are with money?

_____

_____

_____

MONEY STUFF

"My philosophy has always been, do what you love and the money will follow." — Amy Weber

Person B

Are you comfortable talking about money?

_____

What is your opinion of prenuptial agreements?

_____

What was your last big purchase? Was it worth it?

_____

Would you rather spend money on experiences or things?

_____

Are you able to donate to nonprofits?

_____

Do you save for big purchases or use credit?

_____

What was your family's financial situation when you were a kid? How has that influenced how you are with money?

_____

_____

_____

TRIVIA

"What do we live for, if it is not to make life less difficult for each other?" — George Eliot

Person A

Would you rather go camping or to the beach?

_____

How do you feel about breakfast food for dinner?

_____

Are you registered to be an organ donor?

_____

Do you think you could still pass the written portion of the driver's test without studying?

_____

What was your ACT/SAT score?

_____

Do you believe in life on other planets?

_____

If you were forced to sing karaoke, what song would you pick to perform?

_____

_____

TRIVIA

"Relationships end too soon because people stop putting in the
same effort to keep you, as they did to win you." — Unknown

Person B

Would you rather go camping or to the beach?

_____

How do you feel about breakfast food for dinner?

_____

Are you registered to be an organ donor?

_____

Do you think you could still pass the written portion of
the driver's test without studying?

_____

What was your ACT/SAT score?

_____

Do you believe in life on other planets?

_____

If you were forced to sing karaoke, what song would you
pick to perform?

_____

_____

FOOD & DRINK

"All you need is love. But a little chocolate
now and then doesn't hurt." — Charles Schultz

Person A

What do you like on your pizza?

_____

_____

_____

Candlelight dinner or breakfast in bed?

_____

Spicy food: yes or no?

_____

How do you like your coffee?

_____

What are a few food items that you refuse to eat?

_____

_____

_____

What is one thing that you can cook really well?

_____

FOOD & DRINK

"One cannot think well, love well, sleep well, if one has not dined well." — Virginia Woolf, *A Room of One's Own*

Person B

What do you like on your pizza?

_____

_____

_____

Candlelight dinner or breakfast in bed?

_____

Spicy food: yes or no?

_____

How do you like your coffee?

_____

What are a few food items that you refuse to eat?

_____

_____

_____

What is one thing that you can cook really well?

_____

MORE ON FOOD

"My weaknesses have always been food and men—in that order."
— Dolly Parton

Person A

Cake or pie?

_____

What is your guilty pleasure food?

_____

What would you pick as your last meal?

_____

_____

_____

_____

If you could have dinner with any four people who have ever lived, who would you pick?

_____

_____

_____

_____

MORE ON FOOD

"There is no love sincerer than the love of food."
— George Bernard Shaw

Person B

Cake or pie?

_____

What is your guilty pleasure food?

_____

What would you pick as your last meal?

_____

_____

_____

_____

If you could have dinner with any four people who have ever lived, who would you pick?

_____

_____

_____

_____

TRIVIA
"At the touch of love everyone becomes a poet."
— Plato
Person A

What are three habits that you would like to start or stop?

_____

_____

_____

Which goes in the bowl first: cereal or milk?

_____

What is the first thing you noticed about the other person?

_____

_____

Would they rather spend an evening home watching a movie or out on the town?

_____

Preference: cook or clean?

_____

Have you ever secretly read someone's private mail, email, diary, or journal?

_____

TRIVIA

"Who, being loved, is poor?"
— Oscar Wilde, *A Woman of No Importance*

Person B

What are three habits that you would like to start or stop?

_____

_____

_____

Which goes in the bowl first: cereal or milk?

_____

What is the first thing you noticed about the other person?

_____

_____

Would you rather spend an evening home watching a movie or out on the town?

_____

Preference: cook or clean?

_____

Have you ever secretly read someone's private mail, email, diary, or journal?

_____

TRAVEL

"Once a year, go someplace you've never been before."
— Dali Lama

Person A

Do you have a valid passport?

_____

Do you consider yourself to be a light or heavy packer?

_____

What is the longest distance you have traveled? What was the destination?

_____

_____

How do you feel about cruises?

_____

What is a favorite travel memory from your childhood?

_____

_____

_____

_____

TRAVEL
"Never go to bed mad. Stay up and fight."
— Phyllis Diller
Person B

Do you have a valid passport?

_____

Do you consider yourself to be a light or heavy packer?

_____

What is the longest distance you have traveled? What was the destination?

_____

_____

How do you feel about cruises?

_____

What is a favorite travel memory from your childhood?

_____

_____

_____

_____

TRAVEL BUCKET LIST

"Man cannot discover new oceans unless he has the
courage to lose sight of the shore." — Andre Gide

Person A

List the top ten places you would visit if money and
time were not a concern.

1. _____

2. _____

3. _____

4. _____

5. _____

6. _____

7. _____

8. _____

9. _____

10. _____

TRAVEL BUCKET LIST

"The world is a book, and those who do
not travel read only one page." — Saint Augustine

Person B

List the top ten places you would visit if money and
time were not a concern.

1. _____

2. _____

3. _____

4. _____

5. _____

6. _____

7. _____

8. _____

9. _____

10. _____

TRIVIA
"No road is long with good company."
— Turkish Proverb
Person A

What is a favorite guilty pleasure?

_____

_____

What is your morning routine?

_____

_____

_____

_____

What is your least favorite household chore?

_____

_____

When was the last time a movie or something on television made you cry? What was it?

_____

_____

_____

TRIVIA

"A mind that is stretched by new experiences can
never go back to its old dimensions." — Oliver Wendell Holmes

Person B

Do you believe in life on other planets?

_____

_____

What is your morning routine?

_____

_____

_____

What is your least favorite household chore?

_____

_____

When was the last time a movie or something on television
made you cry? What was it?

_____

_____

_____

POLITICAL STUFF

"Lovers don't finally meet somewhere.
They're in each other all along." — Rumi

Person A

Which best describes your feelings about political discussions:

- I would rather not.
- I prefer to discuss them with people whose views are similar to mine.
- I love a good debate.

How old were you the first time you voted?

_____

How have your political views changed over your lifetime?

_____

_____

_____

Have you ever taken part in a march or boycott? If no, what issues could motivate you to join one?

_____

_____

_____

_____

POLITICAL STUFF

"The strongest relationships are between two people who
can live without each other but don't want to." — Harriet Lerner

Person B

Which best describes your feelings about political discussions:

- I would rather not.
- I prefer to discuss them with people whose views are similar to mine.
- I love a good debate.

How old were you the first time you voted?

_____

How have your political views changed over your lifetime?

_____

_____

_____

Have you ever taken part in a march or boycott? If no, what issues could motivate you to join one?

_____

_____

_____

_____

POLITICAL STUFF

"Politics, it seems to me, has been concerned with
right or left instead of right or wrong." — Richard Armour

Person A

When was the last time you voted?

_____

If you found yourself in charge of the entire country,
what are the first five things you would enact or change?

One: _____

_____

Two: _____

_____

Three: _____

_____

Four: _____

_____

Five: _____

_____

POLITICAL STUFF

"In politics stupidity is not a handicap."
— Napoleon Bonaparte

Person B

When was the last time you voted?

_____

If you found yourself in charge of the entire country,
what are the first five things you would enact or change?

One: _____

_____

Two: _____

_____

Three: _____

_____

Four: _____

_____

Five: _____

_____

TRIVIA

"You were worth the wait, and I don't just mean tonight."
— Friends

Person A

Did you ever skip school?

_____

If yes, what did you do during the time you were supposed to be in class?

_____

_____

_____

Psychics: real or a scam? Sought after

_____

Would you rather live in a rural or urban area?

_____

Have you ever cheated on a test?

_____

How do you feel about having kids?

_____

_____

TRIVIA
"Love is a game that two can play and both can win"
— Eva Gabor

Person B

Did you ever skip school?

_____

If yes, what did you do during the time you were supposed to be in class?

_____

_____

_____

Psychics: real or a scam?

_____

Would you rather live in a rural or urban area?

_____

Have you ever cheated on a test?

_____

How do you feel about having kids?

_____

_____

MOVIES, MUSIC, TELEVISION & BOOKS

"But for now, let me say...without hope
or agenda...to me, you are perfect." — *Love, Actually*

Person A

What was your favorite movie when you were a kid?

_____

_____

What three movies do you think you have watched the greatest number of times?

_____

_____

_____

Who would you cast to play yourself in the movie of your life?

_____

What are your favorite genres of music?

_____

_____

_____

_____

MOVIES, MUSIC, TELEVISION & BOOKS

"Anyone can change your life, if you let them."
— The Intouchables

Person B

What was your favorite movie when you were a kid?

_____

_____

What three movies do you think you have watched the greatest number of times?

_____

_____

_____

Who would you cast to play yourself in the movie of your life?

_____

What are your favorite genres of music?

_____

_____

_____

_____

MOVIES, MUSIC, TELEVISION & BOOKS

"If music be the food of love, play on."
— William Shakespeare

Person A

Which decades had the best music?

_____

_____

What are a few favorite songs from your high school years?

_____

_____

_____

_____

What was the first concert you attended? Where was it held and what year did it occur?

_____

_____

What song would you pick as the theme song of your life?

_____

MOVIES, MUSIC, TELEVISION & BOOKS

"Without music, life would be a mistake."
— Friedrich Nietzsche

Person B

Which decades had the best music?

_____

_____

What are a few favorite songs from your high school years?

_____

_____

_____

_____

What was the first concert you attended? Where was it held and what year did it occur?

_____

_____

What song would you pick as the theme song of your life?

_____

MOVIES, MUSIC, TELEVISION & BOOKS

"Whatever our souls are made of, his and mine are the same."
— Emily Brontë, *Wuthering Heights*

Person A

What is the last television show you binge-watched?

_____

_____

If you could be an actor on any television show or movie, past or present, which one would you pick?

_____

_____

What is the last book you read?

_____

What is a favorite book from your childhood or teen years?

_____

What is a book that has positively impacted the way you think, work, or live your life?

_____

_____

MOVIES, MUSIC, TELEVISION & BOOKS

"A painter paints pictures on canvas. But musicians paint their pictures on silence." — Leopold Stokowski

Person A

What is the last television show you binge-watched?

_____

_____

If you could be an actor on any television show or movie, past or present, which one would you pick?

_____

_____

What is the last book you read?

_____

What is a favorite book from your childhood or teen years?

_____

What is a book that has positively impacted the way you think, work, or live your life?

_____

_____

TRIVIA
"Being with you was never an option."
— Unknown
Person A

If you could only have one sense (sight, touch, etc.), which would you pick? Why?

_____

_____

What is your definition of success?

_____

_____

_____

Where would you go, if you could travel back to any place in time?

_____

How should a roll of toilet paper be hung: over or under?

_____

How is one thing that you would you like to learn how to do?

_____

TRIVIA

"If I know what love is, it is because of you."
— Hermann Hesse

Person B

If you could only have one sense (sight, touch, etc.), which would you pick? Why?

_____

_____

What is your definition of success?

_____

_____

_____

_____

Where would you go, if you could travel back to any place in time?

_____

How should a roll of toilet paper be hung: over or under?

_____

What is one thing that you would you like to learn how to do?

_____

TOP TEN MOVIES

"I will never stop trying. Because when you
find the one, you never give up." — *Crazy, Stupid, Love*

Person A

List Your Ten Most Favorite Movies:

1. _____

2. _____

3. _____

4. _____

5. _____

6. _____

7. _____

8. _____

9. _____

10. _____

TOP TEN MOVIES

"That's why they call them crushes. If they were
easy, they'd call 'em something else." — *Sixteen Candles*

Person B

List Your Ten Most Favorite Movies:

1. _____

2. _____

3. _____

4. _____

5. _____

6. _____

7. _____

8. _____

9. _____

10. _____

TOP TEN SONGS

"Music produces a kind of pleasure which
human nature cannot do without." — Confucius

Person A

List Your Ten Most Favorite Songs:

1. _____

2. _____

3. _____

4. _____

5. _____

6. _____

7. _____

8. _____

9. _____

10. _____

TOP TEN SONGS

"Wake up, live your life and sing the melody of your soul."
— Amit Ray

Person B

List Your Ten Most Favorite Songs:

1. _____

2. _____

3. _____

4. _____

5. _____

6. _____

7. _____

8. _____

9. _____

10. _____

BONUS QUESTIONS
"Three words. Eight letters. Say it, and I'm yours."
— *Gossip Girl*

Person A

Do you consider yourself to be an introvert or an extrovert?

_____

What is your favorite thing about yourself?

_____

_____

_____

What are three things that you are grateful for?

_____

_____

_____

What is your fantasy vacation?

_____

_____

_____

_____

BONUS QUESTIONS
"Shared joy is a double joy; shared sorrow is half a sorrow."
— Swedish Proverb

Person B

Do you consider yourself to be an introvert or an extrovert?

_____

What is your favorite thing about yourself?

_____

_____

_____

What are three things that you are grateful for?

_____

_____

_____

What is your fantasy vacation?

_____

_____

_____

_____

MOVIES ABOUT COUPLES

"I miss you Jenny. If there is anything you need,
I won't be far away." — Forest Gump, *Forest Gump*

- City Lights (1931)
- Trouble in Paradise (1932)
- It Happened One Night (1934)
- Top Hat (1935)
- A Night at the Opera (1935)
- Camille (1936)
- The Awful Truth (1937)
- Holiday (1938)
- Bringing Up Baby (1938)
- Ninotchka (1939)
- The Philadelphia Story (1940)
- His Girl Friday (1940)
- The Shop Around the Corner (1940)
- The Lady Eve (1941)
- Casablanca (1942)
- Woman of the Year (1942)
- Brief Encounter (1945)
- An Affair to Remember (1945)
- The Best Years of our Lives (1946)
- Singin' in the Rain (1947)
- The Red Shoes (1948)
- Adam's Rib (1949)

MOVIES ABOUT COUPLES

"You want the moon? Just say the word, and I'll throw a lasso around it and pull it down." —George Baily, *It's a Wonderful Life*

- Born Yesterday (1950)

- An American in Paris (1951)

- The African Queen (1951)

- Pat and Mike (1952)

- Roman Holiday (1953)

- On the Waterfront (1954)

- To Catch a Thief (1955)

- Desk Set (1957)

- Indiscreet (1958)

- Vertigo (1958)

- Pillow Talk (1959)

- Some Like it Hot (1959)

- The Apartment (1960)

- Breakfast at Tiffany's (1961)

- Westside Story (1961)

- Cleopatra (1963)

- Love Story (1970)

- Harold and Maude (1971)

- What's Up, Doc? (1972)

- The Way We Were (1973)

- Annie Hall (1977)

- Grease (1978)

MORE MOVIES ABOUT COUPLES

"You complete me."
— Jerry McGuire, *Jerry McGuire*

- Manhattan (1979)
- Valley Girl (1983)
- Swing Shift (1984)
- Sixteen Candles (1984)
- Splash (1984)
- Out of Africa (1985)
- The Sure Thing (1985)
- Pretty in Pink (1986)
- Something Wild (1986)
- Dirty Dancing (1987)
- Roxanne (1987)
- The Princess Bride (1987)
- Moonstruck (1987)
- Broadcast News (1987)
- Bull Durham (1988)
- Working Girl (1988)
- When Harry Met Sally (1989)
- The Little Mermaid (1989)
- Say Anything (1989)
- Pretty Woman (1990)
- Ghost (1990)
- My Girl (1991)

MORE MOVIES ABOUT COUPLES

"I'm also just a girl, standing in front of a boy,
asking him to love her." — Anna Scott, *Notting Hill*

- Beauty and the Beast (1991)

- Like Water for Chocolate (1992)

- Sleepless in Seattle (1993)

- Dave (1993)

- Groundhog Day (1993)

- Forest Gump (1994)

- Four Weddings in a Funeral (1994)

- Before Sunrise (1995)

- Clueless (1995)

- Love Jones (1995)

- The Bridges of Madison County (1995)

- While You Were Sleeping (1995)

- Jerry McGuire (1996)

- In Love and War (1996)

- The English Patient (1996)

- Titanic (1997)

- As Good as It Gets (1997)

- Fools Rush In (1997)

- Good Will Hunting (1997)

- Hope Floats (1998)

- You've Got Mail (1998)

- How Stella Got Her Groove Back (1998)

MORE MOVIES ABOUT COUPLES

"He is the cheese to my macaroni."
— Diablo Cody, *Juno*

- There's Something About Mary (1998)
- Meet Joe Black (1998)
- 10 Things I Hate About You (1999)
- Notting Hill (1999)
- Forces of Nature (1999)
- Love and Basketball (2000)
- High Fidelity (2000)
- Save the Last Dance (2001)
- Bridget Jones's Diary (2001)
- Serendipity (2001)
- Monsoon Wedding (2001)
- About a Boy (2002)
- Sweet Home Alabama (2002)
- My Big Fat Greek Wedding (2002)
- Something's Gotta Give (2003)
- Big Fish (2003)
- How to Lose a Guy in 10 Days (2003)
- Love Actually (2003)
- Eternal Sunshine of the Spotless Mind (2004)
- The Notebook (2004)
- 50 First Dates (2004)
- A Very Long Engagement (2004)

MORE MOVIES ABOUT COUPLES

"But the you who the you tonight is the same you I was in love with yesterday, the you I'll be in love with tomorrow" — *If I Stay*

- Brokeback Mountain (2005)
- Pride and Prejudice (2005)
- Slumdog Millionaire (2005)
- High School Musical (2006)
- The Lake House (2006)
- Juno (2007)
- Knocked Up (2007)
- Twilight (2008)
- Forgetting Sarah Marshall (2008)
- Up (2009)
- 500 Hundred Days of Summer (2009)
- It's Complicated (2009)
- Date Night (2010)
- Crazy, Stupid, Love (2011)
- The Vow (2012)
- Silver Linings Playbook (2012)
- The Perks of Being a Wallflower (2012)
- The Fault in Our Stars (2012)
- The Hunger Games (2012)
- Great Expectations (2013)
- Blue is the Warmest Color (2013)
- Before Midnight (2013)

MORE MOVIES ABOUT COUPLES

"I would rather share one lifetime with you, than face all the ages of this world alone." — Lord of the Rings

- Her (2013)
- What If (2014)
- Carol (2015)
- Brooklyn (2015)
- Southside With You (2016)
- Loving (2016)
- Me Before You (2016)
- The Shape of Water (2017)
- Our Souls at Night (2017)
- The Big Sick (2017)
- Call Me by Your Name (2017)
- Love, Simon (2018)
- To All the Boys I've Loved Before (2018)
- Cold War (2018)
- A Star is Born (2018)
- Crazy Rich Asians (2018)
- Long Shot (2019)
- Yesterday (2019)
- Always Be My Maybe (2019)
- Yesterday (2019)
- Emma (2020)
- A Secret Love (2020)

RELATIONSHIP PLAYLIST
"Music can name the unnamable and
communicate the unknowable." — Leonard Bernstein

- "Pledging My Love" – Johnny Ace (1954)

- "Only You and You Alone" - The Platters (1955)

- "I Walk the Line" - Johnny Cash (1956)

- "Dream a Little Dream" – Ella Fitzgerald (1956)

- "In the Still of the Night" – The Five Satins (1956)

- "When I Fall in Love" - Nat King Cole (1957)

- "Everyday" - Buddy Holly (1957)

- "Love Me Tender" – Elvis Presley (1957)

- "Chances Are" – Johnny Mathis (1958)

- "The Very Thought of You" - Nat King Cole (1958)

- "I Only Have Eyes for You" - The Flamingos (1959)

- "Put Your Head On My Shoulders" – Paul Anka (1959)

- "At Last" - Etta James (1960)

- "Can't Help Falling in Love" - Elvis Presley (1961)

- "Sealed With a Kiss"- Bryan Hyland (1962)

- "Roses Are Red (My Love) – Bobby Vinton (1962)

- "So Much in Love" - The Tymes (1963)

- "I Only Want To Be With You" – Dusty Springfield (1964)

- "I Want to Hold Your Hand" – The Beatles (1964)

- "The Way You Look Tonight" - Frank Sinatra (1965)

- "I Can't Help Myself" – The Four Tops (1965)

- "I Got You Babe" - Sonny & Cher (1965)

RELATIONSHIP PLAYLIST

"Some days there won't be a song in your heart. Sing anyway."
— Emory Austin

- "Unchained Melody" – The Righteous Brothers (1965)
- "My Girl" – Temptations (1965)
- "When a Man Loves a Woman" – Percy Sledge (1966)
- "God Only Knows" - The Beach Boys (1966)
- "Wild Thing" – The Troggs (1966)
- "How Sweet It Is To Be Loved By – Marvin Gaye (1966)
- "All You Need is Love" – The Beatles (1967)
- "I'm a Believer" - The Monkies (1967)
- "Ain't No Mountain High Enough" – Marvin Gaye (1967)
- "Can't Take My Eyes Off of You" - -Frankie Valli (1967)
- "Dream a Little Dream" – The Mamas & The Papas (1968)
- "This Magic Moment" – The Drifters (1968)
- "Sweet Caroline" - Neil Diamond (1969)
- "Something" – The Beatles (1969)
- "First Time I Ever Saw Your Face" – Roberta Flack (1969)
- "Your Song" – Elton John (1970)
- "I'll Be There" - The Jackson 5 (1970)
- Maybe I'm Amazed" – Paul McCartney (1970)
- "Wild Horses" – Rolling Stones (1971)
- "Let's Stay Together" – Al Green (1971)
- "I Feel the Earth Move" - Carole King (1971)
- "Your Song" - Elton John (1971)

RELATIONSHIP PLAYLIST

"Music is the shorthand of emotion."
— Leo Tolstoy

- "I Saw the Light" – Todd Rundgren (1972)
- "You Are the Sunshine of My Life" – Stevie Wonder (1973)
- "Loves Me Like a Rock" - Paul Simon (1973)
- 'My Love" – Paul McCartney and Wings (1973)
- "Everlasting Love" – Carlton Carl (1974)
- "Lovin' You" - Minnie Riperton (1974)
- "You Are So Beautiful" – Joe Cocker (1974)
- "Annie's Song" – John Denver (1974)
- "This Will Be an Everlasting Love" - Natalie Cole (1975)
- "Love Will Keep Us Together" - Captain & Tennille (1975)
- "You're My Best Friend" – Queen (1976)
- "Still the One" - Orleans (1976)
- "Best of My Love" – Emotions (1976)
- "How Deep is Your Love" - Bee Gees (1977)
- "Just the Way You Are" - Billy Joel (1977)
- "Wonderful Tonight" - Eric Clapton (1977)
- "You Make Loving Fun" – Fleetwood Mac (1977)
- "Hopelessly Devoted to You" - Grease Soundtrack (1978)
- "Just What I Needed" – The Cars (1978)
- "You're the One I Want"- Grease Soundtrack (1978)
- "You Decorated My Life" - Kenny Rogers (1979)
- "Keep on Loving You" - REO Speedwagon (1980)

RELATIONSHIP PLAYLIST

"Without music, life would be a blank to me."
— Jane Austen

- "Don't Stop Believin'" - Journey (1981)
- "Endless Love" – Lionel Ritchie & Diana Ross (1981)
- "Through the Years" - Kenny Rogers (1981)
- "I Melt With You" - Modern English (1982)
- "Islands in the Stream" – Dolly Parton/Kenny Rogers (1982)
- "Only You" – Yaz (1982)
- "Faithfully" – Journey (1983)
- "True" – Spandau Ballet (1983)
- "I Want to Know What Love Is" – Foreigner (1984)
- "Time After Time" - Cyndi Lauper (1984)
- "Hold Me Now" – Thompson Twins (1984)
- "You Give Good Love" - Whitney Houston (1985)
- "Crazy For You" – Madonna (1985)
- "Love Will Conquer All" - Lionel Richie (1986)
- "In Your Eyes" – Peter Gabriel (1986)
- "Take Me Out Tonight" – The Smiths (1986)
- "(I Just) Died in Your Arms" – Cutting Crew (1986)
- "Together Forever" - Rick Astley (1987)
- "I'm Gonna Be (500 Miles) – The Proclaimers (1987)
- "Forever and Ever, Amen" – Randy Travis (1987)
- "Is This Love?" – Whitesnake (1987)
- "Eternal Flame" – The Bangles (1988)

RELATIONSHIP PLAYLIST

"I have found that if you love life,
life will love you back." — Arthur Rubenstein

- "Lovesong" - The Cure (1989)
- "Right Here Waiting" – Richard Marx (1989)
- "Nothing Compares 2U" – Sinéad O'Connor (1990)
- "More Than Words" – Extreme (1990)
- "I'd Love You All Over Again" - Alan Jackson (1990)
- "Unfinished Symphony" - Massive Attack (1991)
- "(Everything I Do) I Do It For You – Bryan Adams (1991)
- "Friday I'm in Love" - The Cure (1992)
- "Harvest Moon" - Neil Young (1992)
- "In This Life" - Collin Raye (1992)
- "I Will Always Love You" – Whitney Houston (1992)
- "Have I Told You Lately?" - Rod Stewart (1993)
- "The Power of Love" – Celine Dion (1993)
- "Anniversary" - Cowboy Junkies (1993)
- "I'll Stand by You" - The Pretenders (1994)
- "When You Say Nothing At All" – Allison Krauss (1994)
- "Always Be My Baby" – Mariah Carey (1995)
- "One Boy, One Girl" - Collin Raye (1995)
- "You Do Something to Me" – Paul Weller (1995)
- "I'm Still in Love With You" - New Edition (1996)
- "Sleepwalking" – Modest Mouse (1996)
- "Truly Madly Deeply" - Savage Garden (1997)

RELATIONSHIP PLAYLIST

"A heart that loves is always young."
— Greek Proverb

- "Everlong" – Foo Fighters (1997)
- "You're Still the One" - Shania Twain (1998)
- "I Don't Want to Miss a Thing" – Aerosmith (1998)
- "In Spite of Ourselves" - John Prine/Iris DeMent (1999)
- "Amazed" - Lonestar (1999)
- "I Knew I Loved You" - Savage Garden (1999)
- "Grow Old With Me" - Mary Chapin Carpenter (1999)
- "Power of Two" - The Indigo Girls (2000)
- "The Luckiest" - Ben Folds (2001)
- "A Thousand Miles" – Vanessa Carlton (2001)
- "True Love Waits" – Radiohead (2001)
- "I Wanna Grow Old With You" - Westlife (2001)
- "Come Away With Me" - Norah Jones (2002)
- "The Blower's Daughter" – Damien Rice (2002)
- "This is the Good Stuff" - Kenny Chesney (2002)
- "Little Moments" – Brad Paisley (2003)
- "Remember When" - Alan Jackson (2003)
- "If I Ain't Got You – Alicia Keys (2003)
- "Crazy in Love – Beyoncé featuring Jay-Z (2003)
- "Such Great Heights" – The Postal Service (2003)
- "Stay With You" - John Legend (2004)
- "Making Memories of Us" – Keith Urban (2004)

RELATIONSHIP PLAYLIST
"Where words fail, music speaks."
— Hans Christian Andersen

- "Inside and Out" – Feist (2004)
- "Breath Me" – Sia (2004)
- "Bless the Broken Road" – Rascal Flatts (2004)
- "First Day of My Life" – Bright Eyes (2005)
- "Do You Remember" - Jack Johnson (2005)
- "I'll Follow You Into the Dark" - Death Cab For Cutie (2005)
- "We Belong Together" - Mariah Carey (2005)
- "Fix You" – Coldplay (2005)
- "Milk & Honey" – As Tall As Lions (2006)
- "My Love" - Justin Timberlake (2006)
- "Hey There Delilah" – (2006)
- "Chasing Cars" – Snow Patrol (2006)
- "Lucky" – Jason Mraz & Colbie Caillat (2006)
- "Falling Slowly – Glen Hansard & Marketa Irgloca (2006)
- "Whatever it Takes" - Lifehouse (2007)
- "Bleeding Love" – Leona Lewis (2007)
- "The Story" - Brandi Carlisle (2007)
- "Awake" – Secondhand Serenade (2007)
- "Love Song" – Sara Bareilles (2007)
- I'm Yours – Jason Mraz (2008)
- "Make You Feel My Love" – Adele (2008)

RELATIONSHIP PLAYLIST

"Don't try to be something to everyone.
Be everything to someone." — Unknown

- "Love Story" – Taylor Swift (2008)
- "Never Say Never" – The Fray (2009)
- "Dog Days Are Over" – Florence and the Machine (2009)
- "Mine" – Taylor Swift (2010)
- "I Keep on Lovin' You" – Reba McEntire (2010)
- "Stuck Like Glue" – Sugarland (2010)
- "Just the Way You Are" – Bruno Mars (2010)
- "We Found Love" – Rhianna w/Calvin Harris (2011)
- "Love You Like a Love Song – Selena Gomez (2011)
- "Love on Top" - Beyoncé (2011)
- "Someone Like You" – Adele (2011)
- "Come Back...Be Here" – Taylor Swift (2012)
- "Still Together" – Mac DeMarco (2012)
- "Hello Sunshine" – Mozella (2012)
- "Little Things" – One Direction (2012)
- "Next to Me" – Emeli Sande´ (2012)
- "Mirrors" – Justin Timberlake (2013)
- "Still Into You" – Paramore (2013)
- "How Long Will I Love You" - Ellie Goulding (2013)
- "Adore You" – Miley Cyrus (2013)
- "Thinking Out Loud" – Ed Sheeran (2014)
- "All of Me" – John Legend (2014)

RELATIONSHIP PLAYLIST

"The best and most beautiful things in this world cannot be seen or even heard—they must be felt with the heart." — Helen Keller

- "Already Home" – A Great Big World (2014)
- "Love Me Like You Do" – Elle Goulding (2015)
- "Love on the Brain" – Rihanna (2016)
- "One Call Away" – Charlie Puth (2016)
- "Perfect" – Ed Sheeran (2017)
- "In Case You Didn't Know"- Brett Young (2017)
- "I'll Name the Dogs" – Blake Shelton (2017)
- "Thinkin Bout You" – Frank Ocean (2018)
- "Shallow" – Bradley Cooper (2018)
- "Butterflies" – Kasey Musgrave (2018)
- "Keep Me Crazy" – Sheppard (2018)
- "Beyond" – Leon Bridges (2018)
- 'Lover" – Taylor Swift (2019)
- "Cuz I Love You" – Lizzo (2019)
- "Just You and I" – Tom Walker (2019)
- "The Bones" – Maren Morris (2019)
- "That's What Love Is" – Justin Bieber (2020)
- "Tattoos Together" – Lauv (2020)
- "U Should" – Chika (2020)
- "POV" – Arianna Grande (2020)
- "Comfortable" – H.E.R. (2020)
- "Stuck With U" – Arianna Grande & Justin Bieber (2020)

The Hear Your Story
Line of Books

At **Hear Your Story**, we have created a line of books focused on giving each of us a place to tell the unique story of who we are, where we have been, and where we are going.

Sharing and hearing the stories of the people in our lives creates closeness, compassion and the cement of knowing each other just a little better.

- Dad, I Want to Hear Your Story; A Father's Guided Journal to Share His Life & His Love

- Mom, I Want to Hear Your Story; A Mother's Guided Journal to Share Her Life & Her Love

- You Chose to Be My Dad; I Want to Hear Your Story: A Guided Journal for Stepdads to Share Their Life Story

- Life Gave Me You; I Want to Hear Your Story: A Guided Journal for Stepmothers to Share Their Life Story

Available at Amazon and all Bookstores

The Hear Your Story
Line of Books

- Grandmother, I Want to Hear Your Story: A Grandmother's Guided Journal to Share Her Life and Her Love

- Grandfather, I Want to Hear Your Story: A Grandfather's Guided Journal to Share His Life and His Love

- Dad Notes: Dad, I Wrote This Book for You

- Mom Notes: I Wrote This Book About the Best Mother Ever

- Love Notes: I Wrote This Book About You

- Because I Love You: The Couple's Bucket List That Builds Your Relationship

- Papá, quiero oír tu historia: El diario guiado de un padre Para compartir su vida y su amor

Available at Amazon and all Bookstores

About the Author

Jeffrey Mason has spent twenty-plus years working with individuals, couples, and organizations to create change, achieve goals, and strengthen relationships.

He begins with the understanding that being human is hard. Jeffrey is fiercely committed to helping others understand that forgiveness is the greatest gift we can give others and ourselves and to remember that while we have eternity, we don't have forever.

Jeffrey would be grateful if you would help people find his books by leaving a review on Amazon. Your feedback helps him get better at this thing he loves.

You can contact him at hello@jeffreymason.com. He would love to hear from you.

Made in the USA
Middletown, DE
22 January 2023

22855772R00066